RIVER always moving

cynthia kozlowski

Azalea Art Press
Southern Pines, North Carolina

ISBN: 978-0-9899961-5-0

Cover engravings from:
Meanderings Among A Thousand Islands
or an Account of Capt. Visger's Daily Trip
on the River St. Lawrence
Time and Reformer Printing and Publishing House, 1884.

contents

Westminster Park

preface

In this first volume of poetry, marking the 80th year of her birth, artist and author Cynthia Kozlowski reveals a portrait of a life in its most condensed essence.

In these poems we find the optimism of childhood; the reverie of a long and fruitful marriage; the grief over a father's addiction and death; meditations on God and religion; and a celebration, above all, of the beauty and mystery of nature.

Life is indeed a "river always moving" and it is my hope that you will find yourself as illuminated and transported by my mother's poems as I have been.

Karen Mireau
December 7, 2013

RIVER always moving

Point Marguerite

When I Awoke In Winter

When I awoke in winter,
it was on the wane.
My boots were worn
from trudging through the snow.
The hills sported bare spots
where my sled refused to go.
The ice rink had ruts that caught my blades,
and often caused a spill.
The snowman in our yard
began to melt as well.

Oh, for another winter!

I would be the first to slide.
I would be the first to skate,
And leave the spots and ruts
to those who would come late.

Devil's Oven

My sense of touch and smell
bring back sweet memories.

On Making Beds

There is a reality in the making of beds.
A pleasurable returning to something that was,
and is again through touch and smell.
The sheets need changing.
They are softened and crinkled,
and filled with odors left from sleep and restless bodies.

I smoothe the sheets.
My fingers flash a message to my brain.
Warm … Drifting … Nest …
Hair … Breast … Entanglement …

I lose my face in a warm limp pillow, and lingering there,
I breathe in love.

Peel Dock

A Drug Addict's Lament

Humanity in rampant rampage
has spread o'er all the breathing ground.

It has twisted up an oak tree here and there
to seek a bit of truth,
but mostly on the ground,
it shades all human forms from any light,
and makes my life on earth as dark as night.

What I seek is covered with the dead debris of ages past,
and living foliage green.

It's hard to push away.

My suffocating spirit still struggling for breath,
lies entwined awaiting
God's great reaper, Death.

Nobby Island

A Man of Means

He walks down the street
his keys dangling and jingling

a key for the car
a key for the boat
a key for the door

He puts the keys in his pocket
feeling serene and secure.
He has paintings of value
all hidden away,
and a Buddha from China
he must look at someday.

take the car to be oiled
take the boat for some grease
have the carpets shampooed
get the chalet subleased,
trim the hedge on the border
and, check to make sure
his accounts are in order

He is so occupied
being a man of such means, that
the wind is a nuisance
the sun is just there
And if God is in heaven,
he doesn't much care.

Warner's Island

*Sunday school teachers
can leave a heavy footprint.*

A Greek Reprimand

The physical is too much with us in our everyday.
When we injure our foot,
Our body moves a different way
To help us limp.

Each part of our physique is so connected.
It twines itself around our soul,
and begs attention like a jealous woman.

It cries,
"I am in pain, ask God to will a cure!"

It shouts,
"I am equal to you, Soul!"

It screams,
"Save me, and you will save yourself!
You cannot leave me!
I will not stand for infidelity!"

We listen, and take heed too many times,
until we intertwine.

We would probably bleed to death,
both of us, were we to tear apart.

Round Island House

My religious beginnings
never quite go away.

We Would Do Well

We would do well to contemplate the tree.
We have a common bond which some have broken.
We find a spot upon the earth,
and plant ourselves quite well.
Some have said we even grow some roots
whereon we dwell.
Transplanting would require major surgery.

We would do well to contemplate the ant.
We have a common bond which some have broken.
We build a house
and work toward its perfection,
until each blade of grass upon our lawn
is directed in an upwardly direction.
Often, it's the opposite direction from ourselves.

We would do well to contemplate the beaver.
We have a common bond which some have broken.
We spy a lovely woody scene beside a flowing stream,
and we must enter it, and conquer all that loveliness,
and make it more a dream.
We improve it with pink patios
and ornamental wrought iron railings,
Cutting down a tree and trimming foliage here and there.
Bare beauty is such an unusable thing.

We would do well to contemplate our God.
We have a common bond which some have broken.

Lake of the Island

Missing the mighty St. Lawrence River
in the Thousand Islands where I grew up.

River Always Moving

Wiry grass rooted in the river's bank,
combed by the rain, and
spilling over the shoreline.

Tiger Lilies sprouting
wild and unarranged from errant seedlings
nurtured here a while back,
now, bending back like acrobats
exposing satin orange clad bellies to the sun.
Like dancers in green leotards,
they quiver in the spritely breeze
that wafts across the deep blue water.

An invisible whisk
beats the water's waves
into peaks of white meringue.
They splash upon the grassy banks,
and smash against the tall grey rocks
sporting a kind of moss psoriasis.

The rocks always still
the river always moving
licking the shore with its moist tongue
again, again, and yet again for a thousand years.

Bonnie Castle

about the author

Cynthia (Garlock) Kozlowski spent her childhood in the small town of Alexandria Bay, New York. There, on the picturesque banks of the St. Lawrence River, she grew deeply attuned with the natural world.

This sensitivity later found expression in many media—from oils to textiles to fine woodworking—as well as in her always artful, whimsical garden designs.

In addition to her work as an artist, Cynthia has written and illustrated numerous picture books, short stories and novels for her four children, her five grandchildren and for her great-granddaughter.

She now divides her time between Florida, New Hampshire and upstate New York—places that greatly inspire her. She continues to write, create and to encourage others to follow their own artistic dreams.

This is her first book of poetry.

The Island Wanderer, 1879

about the illustrations

The engravings in this volume, including the front and back covers, have been reproduced from a booklet titled *Meanderings Among the Thousand Islands or an Account of Capt. Visger's Daily Trip on this River St. Lawrence*, published in Watertown, New York, by the Times and Reformer Printing and Publishing House in 1884. The author is unknown.

Captain Elisha W. Visger

Equal parts travelogue and historical document, it is based on the ship logs of Captain Elisha Washington Visger—a river pioneer born in 1833 and the maternal great-grandfather of the author. It chronicles the twice-daily 40-mile route of the steamship, the *Island Wanderer*, the first of many ships constructed and owned by Captain Visger.

In 1878, Captain Visger built the 100-foot, 150-passenger vessel, *Island Wanderer* (shown on the facing page), after establishing his reputation as a master river pilot at the helm of *The Cygnet*, a river yacht owned by the Northern Navigation Company. He was the first to discover and navigate what is known as "The Lost Channel" on the St. Lawrence River. He later added newer and larger boats to the line, such as *The New Island Wanderer, the Captain Visger* and *the Castinet*, and formed the Alexandria Bay Steamship Company in 1887.

The New Island Wanderer, 1887

The St. Lawrence River, stretching 744 miles between Lake Ontario and the Atlantic Ocean, has been a major thoroughfare for lumber, produce and goods from and to the interior of the U.S. since the early 1800s. The area known as the Thousand Islands embraces an area from Canadian waters near Kingston to Cape Vincent in the United States, and includes over 1700 island formations.

The beauty of its unusual natural panoramas soon attracted wealthy travelers and yachtsmen who had elaborate summer residences and boathouses built of local timber and native stone. The Thousand Islands, abounding with wildlife and sport fish such as small-mouth bass and pickerel, became a favorite of hunters and fishermen. Shipbuilding, fishing tours, hotels, restaurants and construction businesses (including Charles Garlock & Sons, founded by the author's grandfather in 1905) soon grew up around the summer tourist trade.

In May of 1842, Charles Dickens sailed through the area, remarking that:

> The beauty of this noble stream at almost any point, but especially in the commencement of this journey, when it winds its way among the Thousand Islands, can hardly be imagined. The number and constant succession of these islands, all green and richly wooded; their fluctuating sizes, some so large, that for half an hour together, one among them will appear as the opposite bank of the river, and some so small that they are mere dimples on its bosom, their infinite variety of shapes, and the numberless combinations of beautiful forms with trees growing on them, all form a picture fraught with uncommon interest and pleasure.

It appears that Captain Visger may also have possessed a way with words. It was noted that his names and graphic descriptions for some of the previously unexplored areas, such as 'Fiddler's Elbow,' contributed much to the popularity of the Thousand Islands. He continued to operate tour excursions until his retirement in 1894. Captain Visger and his wife, Lavonia McCue Visger, both of whom died in 1915, had two sons: Harmonious Wellington (Will) Visger and Walter LaFayette Visger, who continued the family legacy as shipbuilders and river captains.

The engravings in the book reflect some of the impressive beauty and diversity of the Thousand Islands and of the profound, poetic St. Lawrence River. The remaining illustrations are from vintage postcards or from the personal archives of the author.

The Captain Visger, 1895

Vintage Photos & Post Cards
of Alexandria Bay, New York and Environs

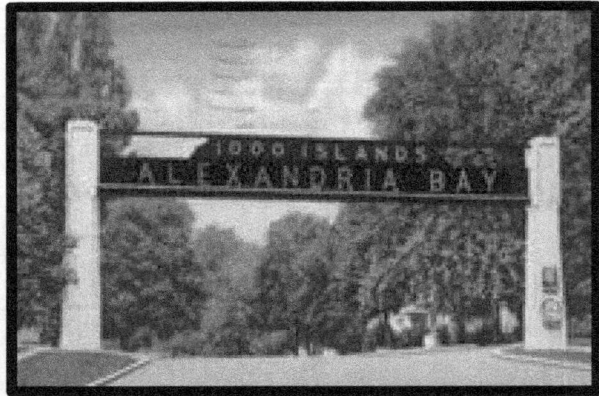

Azalea Art Press
specializes in giving personal attention
to authors who wish to realize
their literary and creative dreams.

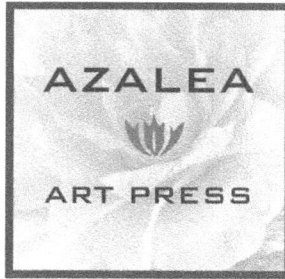

This book of poetry
by Cynthia Kozlowski
may be ordered directly at
www.lulu.com.

To schedule an interview
or signing with the author,
please contact the publisher:

Azalea.Art.Press@gmail.com
azaleaartpress.blogspot.com

www.ingramcontent.com/pod-product-compliance
Lightning Source LLC
LaVergne TN
LVHW091211080426
835509LV00006B/948